Ultimate You!

365 Days to a More Daring,
Deep, and Adorable You

Alison Raine & *Emma Harrison*

Illustrations by James Dignon / Arts Counsel

Scholastic Inc.
New York Toronto London Auckland Sydney
Mexico City New Delhi Hong Kong

ISBN 0-439-11467-5

Distributed under license from
The Petersen Publishing Company, L.L.C.
Copyright © 2001 The Petersen Publishing
Company, L.L.C. All rights reserved.
Published by Scholastic Inc.

 Produced by 17th Street Productions,
an Alloy Online, Inc. company
33 West 17th Street
New York, NY 10011

 Teen is a trademark of Petersen
Publishing Company, L.L.C.

SCHOLASTIC and associated logos are trademarks and/or registered
trademarks of Scholastic Inc.

12 11 10 9 8 7 6 5 4 3 2 1   1 2 3 5 6 7/0

Printed in the U.S.A.
First Scholastic Printing, February 2001

To Liesa, our editor and friend

January

1 It's New Year's Day. Time to start sticking to your resolutions. Don't have any yet? Better write them down. Make at least three that you'll really keep.

If you need extra inspiration to start fresh, pick up a copy of *Catcher in the Rye*. The book's author, J. D. Salinger, was born today in 1919, and the classic, ahead-of-its-time tale about rebel Holden Caulfield will definitely make you think about what you have to be grateful for, and what you want to change.

---

2 Rent *Jerry Maguire*—birthday boy Cuba Gooding, Jr., won an Oscar for his supporting role as Rod Tidwell in the flick. Other lesser-known but high-quality Cuba movies? *Boyz 'N the Hood*, *The Tuskeegee Airmen*, *As Good As It Gets*. Check 'em out.

---

3 Start the year off sweet with this easy ice-cream pie recipe:

ingredients

   1 prepared graham-cracker or Oreo-cookie crust

   8 scoops of ice cream (any flavor), slightly softened

   1 jar prepared chocolate sauce

directions

   1. Preheat oven to 350°F.

   2. Bake the crust for about 10 minutes, or until lightly browned. Let the crust cool.

3. Scoop and spread the ice cream into the crust.

4. Drizzle chocolate sauce over ice cream.

5. Cut into slices and enjoy!

Makes eight servings

---

4 Today is Trivia Day. Sit down with your buds for a game of Trivial Pursuit.

Dare Day! Watch the news. You might learn something. Plus, you can improve your Trivial Pursuit game for next time!

---

5 "Your success has nothing to do with the failure of others."—Ben Affleck
Did you put someone down today? Better come up with a good apology for tomorrow.

Indulge Yourself! To avoid taking your frustration out on someone else in the first place, get your hands on some bubble wrap and pop it all day long. Need more of a release? Lay the bubble wrap down on the floor and dance on it!

---

6 Joan of Arc was born today in 1412. Learn more about this heroine at the cool website www.distinguishedwomen.com. Check out some other fascinating women while you're there.

7 Craft Time!

Stuck inside? Make these cool magnets for your refrigerator or magnetic board. You'll need small circular magnets (pick 'em up at your local craft store); small balsam wood shapes like hearts, squares, circles, stars, etc.; craft paint; glitter; paint markers in assorted colors; and glue. Paint each of your wood shapes with a base color. Make sure you paint both sides, waiting for one side to dry before you flip it over and paint the other. Once the paint is dry, use the paint markers to write sayings on the shapes. You can put just your name, your favorite movie quote, or a phrase that inspires you. Let the paint marker dry, then use a dab of glue to attach the shapes to the magnets.

Party of the Month:
Summer Soiree

Yes, you heard right! It may be January, but this is a surefire way to beat the winter blahs.

Invite: A slew of your best friends.

Dress: Like you're headed for a Hawaiian luau. Have everyone wear bathing suits and shorts and grab a bunch of those cheesy plastic leis. (Make sure you crank up the heat in your house.)

Treats: Lemonade, iced tea, frozen fruit drinks, ice cream, hot dogs, whatever your favorite summer treats are.

Games/activities: Limbo! Have a pie-eating contest. Play a tape of ocean sounds and blast a reggae CD.

If you're really ambitious: Get a sandbox or kiddy pool and fill it up with sand. (This is if you have some very cool parents!) Scare up some of that colorful sunblock and paint one another's faces.

8

It's Elvis Presley's birthday! Grab one of the King's CDs and swivel your hips like they've never been swiveled before!

Indulge Yourself! You're probably hungry from all that dancing, so make s'mores at home in your microwave (but don't put them in for too long or the marshmallows will explode!).

9

Health Tip: Heading for your favorite fast-food joint after school with your friends? Order something broiled or baked, rather than something fried.

Backstreet Boy A. J. McLean was born today in 1978, so blast some BSB tunes on the car ride over.

10 *Friendship Tip:* Make a pact with a friend to try something new that she likes to do. Then she can return the favor. You might discover some new interests!

11 Need someone to talk to but can't share your secret with friends from school? Check out www.teenchat.net and spill your guts with some new anonymous pals.

Beauty Boost! Has all that typing shown you that you have a bad case of brittle winter nails? Strengthen them with a clear nail-hardening polish.

12 Here's an evening activity for you. Get some friends together and have a snowball fight . . . unless you live in Arizona, in which case a water gun fight might be more up your alley.

13 Michael Jordan announced his retirement on this day in 1999. Play a game of pickup basketball in his honor.

Hungry from all that running around? Make this tasty and healthy Japanese miso soup for National Soup Month:

ingredients
 ¹/₃ cup miso
 ¹/₂ pound tofu, cut into small cubes (both of these

items can be found in Asian specialty markets or natural foods stores)

5 cups water

directions

1. Boil the water in a saucepan. Turn the heat down low and in a separate bowl, mix a cup of the water with the miso. Whisk until smooth.

2. Pour the miso and water back into the saucepan and add the tofu. Stir a couple of times and let the soup sit for a minute before serving.

Makes 4 servings

14

Feeling less than confident? Sit down and make a list of ten things you like about yourself.

Friendship Tip: Now that you've raised your confidence quotient, do your friend a favor and boost hers. Write her a note (no e-mails allowed!) and let her know all the reasons she's so awesome.

Ever thought your cat would look cute in a skirt? Today is National Dress Up Your Pet Day. (We're not kidding!)

15 In honor of Martin Luther King, Jr. Day this month, check out a copy of his famous "I Have a Dream" speech and get inspired.

16 *Try Something New!* **January is National Hobby Month, so pick up a new pastime like bowling, tarot card reading, or bocce ball. If you end up really loving the activity, start a club with friends to enjoy your new hobby weekly or monthly.**

17 Have you ever tried to stand on your head? Why not do it—and then think about a problem that's been bugging you from an upside-down perspective. You never know what you'll come up with!

18 Today is Winnie-the-Pooh Day. Read *The Tao of Pooh* and cuddle up with your Tigger doll.

Indulge Yourself! While you're regressing, do some more of your favorite childhood activities, like playing jacks, jumping rope, or finger painting. Love your inner child!

19 *Dare Day!* Stand up for something you truly believe in. For example, do the girls' sports teams in your school get enough coverage in the paper? If not, start up a newsletter letting everyone know how much the girls' teams rock!

20 All your favorite shows are in reruns until February sweeps. So read a book! Check out the teen section on Amazon.com for all the latest and greatest reads. And if your eyes get dried out from all that reading, here's a quick solution: Take some chamomile tea bags, place them in hot water, let them cool, and then place the tea bags over your eyes for 15 minutes.

---

21 *Astrology Alert!* If you were born between today and February 19, you're an Aquarius, which means that you have strong convictions and will fight for what you believe in. Your ideal love matches are Aries, Gemini, Sagittarius, and Libra.

Today is National Hugging Day. Hug someone you've never hugged before.

---

22 *Get Involved!* Do some research on your local politicians. Hey—one day you'll be able to vote!

Dare Day! Watch a romantic flick, then get inspired and make some serious eye contact with a cutie.

23 *Friendship Tip:* Frame a special photo of you and a friend and give it to her as a gift.

24 *Indulge Yourself!* Eat some raw cookie dough and chase it down with a big glass of milk.

25 Borrow your best friend's clothes and dress like she does. Today is Opposite Day.
The famous writer Virginia Woolf—a feminist before her time—was born on this day in 1882. Do something with just the girls in her honor.

26 "G'day, mate!" Today is Australia Day. Try some Vegemite—a truly Aussie delicacy—on toast.
Actress Sara Rue from the WB's *Popular* celebrates her birthday today.

27 Wear socks that don't match under long pants or boots—no one but you will know about your little rebellion.

28 *Beauty Boost!* If you're sick of your old accessories, spice up a boring plastic headband by decorating it with colorful beads. All you have to do is snag a bag of pretty beads and a glue gun at your local craft store and get creative.

Big birthday day! Actor Elijah Wood, Nick Carter of the Backstreet Boys, and 'N Sync's Joey Fatone were all born today.

---

29 Craving some Fritos? You're in luck! Today is National Corn Chip Day.

Oprah Winfrey was born on this day in 1954. So while you're chomping on your chips, pick up her magazine, *O*, at your local newsstand and boost up on girl power!

---

30 *That '70s Show*'s Wilmer Valderrama has a birthday today—why don't you and your friends try speaking with a random foreign accent, like his character, Fez, does? (No one on the show knows where Fez is really from!)

---

31 Make a big batch of popcorn today— National Popcorn Day! For something different, throw some grated cheese or garlic salt on top.

'N Sync member Justin Timberlake was born today in 1981.

February

1 Invite your friend over for a sleepover and watch the tube. *Late Night with David Letterman* premiered on this night in 1982. Up for an all-nighter? Then pop the classic flick *Gone with the Wind* into the VCR. The film's legendary star Clark Gable was born on this day in 1901.

2 Today is Groundhog Day. Make sure you find out if the furry guy saw his shadow and then rent the comedy *Groundhog Day*.

3 Did you floss today? February is Dental Health Month. Flossing every day helps to prevent tooth decay and gum disease—and also keeps your smile beautiful!

Toothbrush check: Your toothbrush should be changed every four to six months (or after you've been sick).

4 It's African American History Month. Read up on heroes like Rosa Parks, Jackie Robinson, and the "Little Rock Nine."

5 Searching for a valentine? Make a list of all the guys you've ever had a crush on . . . one of those cuties might fit the bill.

Still looking for the perfect guy? List five qualities your future boyfriend should have. Then make a list of five reasons your dream guy will fall for you.

6 Play a game of catch in honor of baseball legend Babe Ruth's birthday.

Indulge Yourself! Enough sports for one day—get back in touch with your funky side by shutting your bedroom door, blasting your favorite song, and dancing around your room.

---

7 Listen to some good ol' country music and kick up your heels with a little line dancing in honor of Garth Brooks's birthday. Not your thing? Then get groovy—Ashton Kutcher of *That '70s Show* was born today in 1978.

---

8 "I try to choose the most interesting characters, but I think it might be interesting to play a character that's alarmingly normal."—Seth Green
Watch all of your *Buffy* videotapes to celebrate Seth's birthday.

But don't stay inside watching the tube for too long—it's Kite-Flying Day, so get on out there and play!

9

Gear up for Valentine's Day by making some fudge for your sweetie . . . or your friends.

ingredients

- 3 16–ounce packages semisweet chocolate chips
- 1 14–ounce can sweetened condensed milk
- 1 ½ teaspoons vanilla extract
- ½ cup chopped nuts
- 1 cup mini-marshmallows

directions

1. Line an 8 x 8 or a 9 x 9 pan with waxed paper. Set aside.
2. In a big saucepan, melt the chocolate chips with the condensed milk over low heat.
3. Remove from heat and stir in the vanilla extract, chopped nuts, and mini-marshmallows.
4. Spread the mixture evenly into pan. Chill for 2 hours or until fudge is firm.
5. Turn pan over onto a cutting board, peel off the waxed paper, and cut fudge into squares.
6. Enjoy! (To keep fudge for a few days, wrap well and refrigerate.)

Makes approximately 12 squares of fudge

10

Dare Day! Surprise your parents and take out the garbage.

Party of the Month: Swingin' Singles Party

It's the anti-Valentine's Day bash. Sort of.

Invite: A small-ish group of your closest friends. Every guy has to bring a platonic female friend and every girl has to bring a platonic male friend. This way there will be plenty of unattached folks to meet . . . and maybe someone will even make a love connection.

Dress: Kinda dressy yet still comfy. Nice pants or skirts for girls. Pants and nice shirts for guys. (Call it casual chic if you want to be sophisticated about it.)

Treats: Red fruit punch, finger foods, heart-shaped cakes, candy hearts, red hots.

Games/activities: Spin the bottle, would you rather, seven minutes in heaven. Have everyone bring his or her choice for the best love song or movie of all time.

If you're really ambitious: Scour the magazines this month to find a compatibility quiz, then give them to your friends. Every matched couple has to hang and chat for ten minutes.

11

Friendship Tip: Clue in a lovelorn guy pal on the secret lives of girls . . . but don't tell him everything!

Brandy's sitting on top of the world today—her birthday.

12

Need a way to bond with Mom? Rent birthday girl Christina Ricci's first movie, *Mermaids,* and watch it together, just the two of you.

It's Abraham Lincoln's birthday. Take a tour of the White House at www.whitehouse.gov/WH/kids/html /home.html and learn more about the nation's capital.

13

Hate your name? Invent a new one—today is Get a Different Name Day (no joke).

Dare Day! Complete your personal makeover by temporarily dyeing your hair or giving yourself a bunch of henna tattoos.

14

Today is Valentine's Day. Make old-school valentines with construction paper and lace doilies for all your friends and family. Hand them out with goody bags filled with Hershey's Kisses, conversation hearts, and red hot candies.

No date for the big day? Why don't you and all of your single friends have dinner together?

15 Brian Littrell and Kevin Richardson of the Backstreet Boys announced their engagements on this day in 2000. Mourn by putting "Show Me the Meaning of Being Lonely" on replay. Or cheer yourself up instead by getting in touch with your inner child and playing a game of Candy Land with your friends in honor of National Gumdrop Day.

---

16 The best way to get back at someone who's been mean to you is to do something nice in return. So smile at your enemies for Do a Grouch a Favor Day.

---

17 Hit the ice! The U.S. Women's Hockey Team won the gold in Nagano, beating Canada 3–1 on this day in 1998.

Jerry O'Connell was born today in 1974. Rent *Stand by Me* and see what the actor looked like in his awkward years. (See, everyone has 'em!)

---

18 Ever felt so frustrated about something you wanted to explode? Well, that could be messy. Try going for a walk or a run instead. Exercise is great for getting out aggression. Since today's John Travolta's birthday, you could even listen to the classic *Grease* sound track while you jog— you'll feel much better.

19 Take the initiative and organize a family trip to the movies, then break out the Junior Mints in the theater—it's Chocolate Mint Day. (We're not kidding!)

20 *Astrology Alert!* If you were born between today and March 20, you're a Pisces, which means you're sensitive and creative . . . and, of course, you like water! Your ideal love matches are Taurus, Capricorn, Scorpio, and Cancer.

Roswell's Majandra Delfino was born today in 1981 and the Backstreet Boys' Brian Littrell in 1975.

21 Grab some tarot cards and learn your destiny in honor of Card Reading Day. Even if you now know your future, you still have to live in the present. So grab a mic and belt out some tunes like actress/songstress Jennifer Love Hewitt, who celebrates her birthday today.

22 *Get Involved!* Do something positive for your community like participating in a walk for charity or lending a hand at your local hospital. Check out the many possibilities at www.teenvolunteernow.org.

Still have some time left over? Make yourself a personal time capsule. List all of your favorite things from best friends to favorite radio station and biggest pet peeve. Put it away until next year and see how you've changed (or not!). Make it a habit and keep a capsule every year.

We know you're not a bragger anyway, but make sure you don't slip up today of all days—it's Humble Day.

23

Today is National Tortilla Chip Day. Impress your friends and make some yummy guacamole to go with those chips—it's easy!

ingredients

   2 ripe avocados
   1 tomato, chopped
   1 onion, minced
   the juice of one lime
   salt and pepper to taste

directions

1. Peel avocados and mash them in a small to medium mixing bowl.
2. Stir in the tomato, onion, half of the lime's juice, and salt and pepper.
3. Taste—add more lime juice and salt and pepper if you desire.
4. Break open the chips and serve!

24 "You always think you're in love, but then when you fall out of love, you go, 'That wasn't love.' You have to think that true love is the kind of thing that you won't fall out of."
—Casey Affleck, Ben's little brother

Get your heart trashed lately? You will get over him. We promise.

Indulge Yourself! **Read a bad romance novel to help the healing process.**

---

25 Check out a book on Pierre-Auguste Renoir and take in his famous, beautiful impressionist paintings. He was born today in 1841.

Health Tip: Don't be a statistic. According to the George H. Gallup International Institute, about two out of three teenage smokers say they want to quit, and 70 percent say that if they could choose again, they'd never start smoking.

---

26 Have a nutty snack on National Pistachio Day and wear your fave jeans today to celebrate Levi Strauss's birthday.

---

27 Go to the zoo and check out some fuzzy friends on International Polar Bear Day.

Health Tip: Want your hair to look as thick and shiny as the cuddly bears' coats? Eat foods rich in silicon, such as bell peppers, apples, leafy green vegetables, and beets, to get great shine.

---

28 Go ahead—fall asleep in the library. Today is Public Sleeping Day. Or, if you're having trouble sleeping, try a cup of soothing Sleepytime tea, and you'll nod off in no time.

Felicity's Tangi Miller celebrates her birthday today.

---

29 If it's a leap year, then you get an additional day of February today! Use the extra hours to do one of those things that you're always complaining you never have time for, like an all-out aerobic routine or some peaceful meditation.

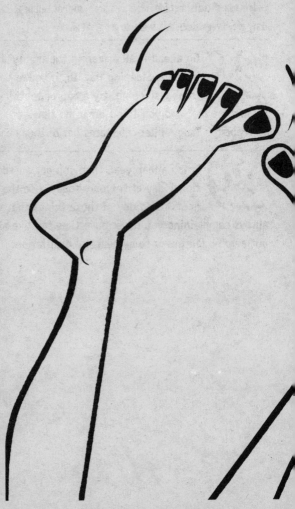

March

1 Make your own peanut butter* in honor of Peanut Butter Lovers' Month. It's easy!

ingredients

- 1 ½ cups roasted, unsalted peanuts
- 1 tablespoon peanut oil

directions

1. Mix the peanuts with the peanut oil in a bowl.
2. Pour the mixture into a food processor and blend until the mixture's very smooth. (Never bothered with the food processor before? Just ask Mom or Dad to show you how.)
3. Spread onto some bread, apples, or celery and enjoy! (The peanut butter will be good for two weeks in the fridge.)

   * Recipe from the Girl Power website at www.health.org/gpower/

Health Tip: Peanut butter is a great source of protein, which is necessary for the growth and maintenance of body structures.

Wacky peanut butter fact: Peanut shells are used to make animal feed, kitty litter, and fuel for power plants.

---

2 Lavender's the most soothing of scents. Grab some lavender-scented spray from Bath & Body Works and spritz your pillow. Or light a lavender-scented candle to help destress yourself.

March

Dare Day! **Now that you're feeling nice and calm, spread it around. Get chatty with someone you've never talked to before.**

3 *Friendship Tip:* **Bring a batch of cookies to share with your friends at lunch. Remember what month it is—you could bring peanut butter cookies!**

Party of the Month: *Spa time!*

After all the coupledom running rampant in February, it's time for you to chill with your *chicas*. No guys allowed for this time-of-your-life sleepover.

Invite: **A few fun-loving girls.**

Dress: **Your most comfy sleepwear.**

Treats: **Fresh fruit and veggies, pretzels, frozen yogurt.**

Games / activities: **Makeovers, manicures, pedicures, facials, personality and friendship quizzes.**

If you're really ambitious: **Rent an instructional yoga video and follow along. You and your friends will be in for some serious, relaxing slumber.**

4 March is National Nutrition Month. If you don't already, you should start chowing down on whole-grain breads and cereals, dried beans and peas, and fruits and vegetables. These fiber-rich foods may reduce your risk of cancer and heart disease.

5 "A women's place is in the House—and in the Senate." —Gloria Schaffer, political activist
Head to the library or your local bookstore and pick up a copy of *Stay True: Short Stories for Strong Girls* or *Girls Speak Out: Finding Your True Self* in honor of Women's History Month.

6 *Friendship Tip:* Know that secret you're dying to tell? Don't.

7 Invite some friends over and have a Monopoly party. The board game was invented on this day in 1933.

Beauty Boost! After you're finished with the game, spend some time in front of the mirror experimenting with different eye shadows.

8 Freddie Prinze, Jr. and James Van Der Beek were both born on this day, exactly a year apart— Freddie in 1976, and James in 1977. Follow up a viewing of *She's All That* with *Varsity Blues*.

March

9 *Health Tip:* **Don't get sick!** Prevent germs from spreading and infecting you by always washing your hands before eating.

---

10 Can you imagine a world without telephones? Alexander Graham Bell invented the phone on this day in 1876. To celebrate this anniversary, spend shameless hours on the phone today.

---

11 March is National Youth Arts Month. Try some of these crafty activities to get your creative juices flowing:

• Design a greeting card on the computer and e-mail it to a friend.

• Pick up an origami book and try out the art of Japanese paper folding.

• Grab a sketchbook and sit down in front of any object you choose. Now, turn the object upside down to see it from a whole new angle and sketch it—you'll be surprised at how amazing it turns out!

---

12 Jack Kerouac, the Beat generation author of *On the Road*, was born on this day in 1921. So take a tip from his wanderer spirit and go for a walk, will ya?

Try Something New! **After getting back from that walk, play a game of chess. If you don't know how to play, devote some time to learning.**

---

13 "Life moves pretty fast; if you don't stop and take a look around once in a while you could miss it." —Ferris Bueller

Take a moment to appreciate everything you have today. And remember that there are others who aren't so lucky. Want to help those in need but don't know how? Start small. Go to www.thehungersite.com and click on the "donate free food" button. The United Nations World Food Program will donate a meal to a hungry person every time you click it—up to once a day.

---

14 Eat those chips and don't feel guilty. After all, it's National Potato Chip Day.

Actor Chris Klein celebrates his birthday. Hmm. Wonder if he likes chips . . .

---

15 *Friendship Tip:* Go back to your favorite childhood park with a friend and play on the swings.

---

16 *Get Involved!* Ask your grandparents or oldest living relative about your family's history. If you're feeling really ambitious you could put it down on paper with old family photographs and create a scrapbook to be handed down through the generations.

March

17 Wear green today in honor of St. Patrick's Day.

You may not have a leprechaun's pot of gold right now, but one day you could come close if you start saving two dollars a week.

---

18 You've heard all about it, now find out the real deal on feng shui and rearrange your room for a better 'tude. Check out *Do-It-Yourself Feng Shui* at your local bookstore. Quick tip: Make sure your bed is facing the North/South compass directions to ensure a good night's sleep.

---

19 Time for some spring cleaning. Organize your closet so that you can actually find things. Put all of your shirts together, all of your pants together, and so on. And move all non-seasonal stuff to the back. Getting dressed will be a lot easier!

And then continue on by cleaning out your locker at school. Throw away or recycle anything that you definitely don't need anymore. Need some tips on recycling? Go to www.epa.gov/recyclecity/

20 Spring begins today!

Want a change of pace? Make a list of five new outdoor activities to try, then go for it!

Still bored with your everyday existence? Try out a new shampoo or body soap or invent a different wake-up routine. Sometimes small variations can make a big difference!

---

21 *Astrology Alert!*
If you were born between today and April 20, you're an Aries, which means you're outspoken and enthusiastic. Your ideal love matches are Aquarius, Gemini, Leo and Libra.

Today is Fragrance Day. Hit the mall and test out the latest perfumes. Some good scent ingredients for fiery Aries: musk, jasmine, and sandalwood.

---

22 It's National Goof Off Day, so there's no need to feel guilty if you kick back, stare at the stars, and daydream for at least an hour. But if you have energy to burn, play a game of hoops with your girlfriends to celebrate the fact that the first women's college basketball game was played on this day in 1893.

23 Actress Keri Russell of *Felicity* was born today in 1976. Let her daring spirit (remember the big haircut?!) inspire you to make a bold move of your own.

---

24 Feeling wiped out? Try sniffing citrus-, jasmine-, or peppermint-scented candles for a sudden energy boost.

Health Tip!
Sometimes you actually need to use energy to get more. If you give yourself an intense workout every morning for a week, we bet you'll start feeling much more alert!

---

25 Have waffles for breakfast! Today is Waffle Day.

Indulge Yourself! Spend hours surfing the Net after school today. Then if you get too restless, try for a slam dunk in honor of WNBA player Sheryl Swoopes's birthday.

26

Never eat the green stuff? Well, today is Spinach Festival Day. Try this recipe for spinach dip and we promise you'll have a whole new appreciation for the veggie:

ingredients

1 10–ounce package of frozen chopped spinach (thawed)

1 cup onion, minced

1 clove garlic, minced

1 teaspoon ground cumin

1 cup cucumber, minced

$1/2$ cup sour cream

$1/2$ cup low-fat mayonnaise

Salt and pepper to taste

directions

1. Squeeze the water out of the spinach and put spinach into a mixing bowl.
2. Mix in the onion, garlic, cumin, cucumber, sour cream, and mayonnaise.
3. Season with salt and pepper to taste.
4. Let dip stand at room temperature for 1 hour and stir again before serving.
5. Serve with veggies or pita bread and enjoy!

27

Beauty Boost! Want glossy locks? After you rinse out your conditioner, squeeze the juice from a few lemons into your hair, then rinse with cool water. You'll be shining in no time!

March

Singer Mariah Carey has a birthday today. Break some glasses trying to mimic her high notes.

---

28 *Health Tip:* Keep those bones strong by consuming 1,200 mg of calcium today—and every day. Calcium can be found in low-fat milk products, dark green leafy vegetables, and calcium-fortified juices and grains.

---

29 "I don't know the key to success, but the key to failure is trying to please everybody." —Bill Cosby

Feel like you're being pulled in all different directions? Choose one and go with it. You'll feel much better and you'll accomplish a lot more.

---

30 *Indulge Yourself!* Watch a sappy movie and weep like crazy. Be sure to keep a box of tissues nearby.

Beauty Boost! Eyes puffy from all the crying? Cut thin slices of raw potato and hold them over your eyelids for at least ten minutes. Voila! You've been depuffed!

---

31 Get into the spirit of spring. Commune with nature by starting your own garden, or even smelling a couple flowers from your neighbor's.

April

1 Watch out! Today is April Fools' Day. In the spirit of the day, make a list of harmless practical jokes and then play one on an unsuspecting friend.

2 National Peanut Butter and Jelly Day gives you a great excuse to enjoy some PB&J for lunch today. It's also Hans Christian Andersen's birthday. Why don't you try to write your very own fairy tale? Or modernize a classic fairy tale instead, giving the story your own spin.

3 Interesting tidbit: In Kentucky you can see something called a "moon-bow," a rainbow that's visible only at night! Check it out on-line if you can't visit the state in person!

4 Having trouble making a big decision? Sit down and make a list of pros and cons, ask advice from someone you trust, and then listen to your heart. You'll figure it out!

5 *Friendship Tip:* Don't roll your eyes when she starts talking about her crush . . . again.

6 Legendary magician Harry Houdini was born on this day in 1874. Pick up a magic book and try your hand at a few tricks.

April

7 *Health Tip:* Improve your posture! It's better for you, and you'll look better, too! Make an effort to stand with your head up, chest out, and back straight—you'll be amazed at how much more confident you'll look and feel. Also, remember to always wear your backpack on both shoulders.

---

8 Today is Astronomy Day. Look up at the sky tonight and try to find the constellations.

---

9 *Never Been Kissed* premiered on this day in 1999. How about renting the flick and then making the effort to talk to someone in school you've never spoken to before?

---

10 Do something nice for your brother or sister in honor of National Siblings Day.

---

11 *Dare Day!* April is the month for showers. So go outside and sing in the rain. Splash in some puddles while you're at it!

---

12 Feeling out of touch with faraway friends or family? Start a monthly e-mail newsletter to fill them in on what's going on with you and ask them to do the same. You'll be all caught up in no time!

Party of the Month: *Lotsa Laughs*

April's known for being a down and drippy month. Liven it up with a comedy party. No frowns allowed!

Invite: Tons of fun-loving friends. Everyone must bring at least one of his or her favorite jokes.

Dress: It's all about clashing at a comedy party. Mix colors, fabrics, and patterns as part of the decorating scheme.

Decorations: Go wild with color. A rainbow of balloons, streamers, glitter, and confetti.

Treats: Bizarre recipes.

Games/ activities: Have everyone get up and tell their joke, then judge the best joke by the audience's applause. Have a prize for your funniest friend.

If you're really ambitious: Go improv and act out your own version of the TV show *Whose Line Is It Anyway?* Make up wacky scenarios and then have one another act them out on the spot.

13

Need something sweet in your life? Make these magic cookie bars*:

ingredients

$^1/_2$ cup butter

1 cup graham-cracker crumbs

1 can Eagle Brand sweetened condensed milk

1 6-oz. package chocolate chips

1 $3^1/_2$-oz. package flaked coconut

1 cup chopped walnuts

directions

1. Preheat oven to 350°F (325°F if using a glass pan).

2. Melt the butter in a saucepan over low heat.

3. Sprinkle graham-cracker crumbs over the butter.

4. Pour sweetened condensed milk evenly over crumbs.

5. Top evenly, first with chocolate chips, then coconut, then walnuts. Press down gently.

6. Bake 25–30 minutes or until lightly browned.

(Psst! Hey—remember to turn off the oven when you're done—you don't wanna burn the house down.)

Cool thoroughly before cutting.

* This is an Eagle Brand® recipe

Eagle Brand® is a registered trademark of Borden, Inc.

14 *Get Involved!* Help build a much-needed house with Habitat for Humanity, or at least explore their awesome website at www.habitat.org, in honor of Sarah Michelle Gellar's birthday. It's the actress's favorite charity.

---

15 *Health Tip:* Breakfast is the most important meal of the day, so don't skip out. That cereal or yogurt gives you energy to keep you going. Orange juice is a natural boost, so chug some of that instead of coffee.

Make a list of five things your mom makes you eat that you hate. Then try to think of other foods you could eat to substitute that would make your mom and you happy.

---

16 Today is Stress Awareness Day. Feeling tense? Take a time-out and relax by lounging in a hot bubble bath while listening to your favorite album. Stay  in the tub till your fingers prune! Then check out www.yogasite.com for tips on great relaxation exercises.

---

17 *Friendship Tip:* After school, hit the mall with a friend and a Polaroid camera and take shots of each other in silly getups.

Try Something New! **Stop into a musical instrument store and learn a few chords on the guitar in honor of International Guitar Month.**

18 If you're brave, you might want to give juggling a shot today—it's International Jugglers' Day.

It's also Melissa Joan Hart's birthday, which makes sense since the talented actress does a great job juggling her roles on TV and in movies!

19 Make some garlic bread and ward off those vampires for Garlic Day . . . just don't go kissing anybody afterward!

20 *Beauty Boost!* **Don't like to wear a lot of eye makeup? Try a good thickening mascara by itself—it'll really open up your eyes.**

21 *Astrology Alert!* **If you were born between today and May 21, you're a Taurus, which means you're practical and determined. Your ideal love matches are Pisces, Capricorn, Cancer, and Scorpio.**

22 Which flavor Jelly Belly is your favorite? Today, National Jelly Bean Day, is the day to taste 'em all and find out. Continue to sweeten your day by wearing some flavored lip gloss.

Get Involved! Use your determination to organize a group to clean up your local park in honor of Keep America Beautiful Month.

---

23 Read one of the most famous love stories of all time—*Romeo and Juliet*. Playwright William Shakespeare is believed to have been born on this day in 1564.

Friendship Tip: Let the tragedy inspire you to tell everyone in your life how much he or she means to you.

---

24 *Health Tip:* Don't rush meals—it's bad for digestion. Take your time and enjoy your food. If you find yourself eating too fast, put your fork down in between bites and take a breather.

---

25 Today is Professional Secretaries' Day. Bring your school secretary a little gift. Hey, it's not a bad idea to have him or her on your side, is it?

---

26 *Dare Day!* Ask your parents or grandparents how they met and listen to the whole darn story.

April

Beauty Boost! Do some spring cleaning and go through your makeup drawer. Chuck all of last season's colors and any expired products to make room for some fun new beauty items.

---

27 It's Tell a Story Day. Sit down with some friends and give the first line to a story. Go around in a circle and have everyone else add on until you finish. Who knows? You might end up with a masterpiece!

---

28 Today is Great Poetry Reading Day. Go to the library and check out some poetry. (Make sure it's great!)

---

29 "Surely it's better to sleep late in the morning only when it's a rare privilege, not an everyday occurrence." —Lauren Bacall

Take Lauren's advice and relish your time in bed this morning.

It's Jerry Seinfeld's birthday . . . not that there's anything wrong with that.

---

30 Bored with your locks? Go get 'em cut today—Hairstylist Appreciation Day. You should try to give your hair a trim every six weeks to keep your strands healthy.

Actress Kirsten Dunst and Jeff Timmons of 98° share a birthday today, but he was born nine years before she was, in 1973.

National Good

National Good Car Care Month

May

1 It's May Day. Observe the holiday any way you like—even if it's just by flashing your friends extra-wide smiles!

Actors Uma Thurman and Ethan Hawke celebrate their wedding anniversary today. Rent *Gattaca*, the movie they were working on when they fell in love.

---

2 In honor of National Physical Fitness Month, start an exercise routine today. According to the President's Council on Physical Fitness and Sports, regular exercise and participation in sports can reduce girls' risk for obesity, reduce symptoms of stress and depression, and improve self-esteem.

---

3 "Going to the movies alone is one of the most pleasurable things I do." —model/actress Tyra Banks

Take a tip from Tyra and catch one of the new spring flicks on your own.

---

4 *Dare Day!* Go the whole day without wearing a watch.

'N Sync's Lance Bass has a birthday today.

---

5 Today is Cinco de Mayo (translation—the fifth of May), which marks the victory of the Mexican army over the French at the Battle of Puebla.

May

Celebrate by chowing down on some quesadillas!

6 For Beverage Day today, whip up a refreshing batch of lemonade to quench your thirst.

While you sip the delicious drink, flip through a dream analysis book—or look for a site on the Internet—and try to interpret your latest dream. Sigmund Freud, the father of psychoanalysis and a leader in dream interpretation, was born on this day in 1856.

7 It's that time of year again . . . Mother's Day is approaching! Buy your mom a book, then make her a special bookmark to go with it. You'll need colorful ribbon, about one inch thick, and scissors. With the scissors, fringe the edges of the ribbon. Decorate, and voilà! You have a bookmark.

8 Go barefoot—today is No Socks Day! (No joke.) Learn to samba (barefoot, of course)! It's Enrique Iglesias's birthday!

9 *Get Involved!* Wanna save a life one day? Learn CPR.

And speaking of helping others, why not help yourself? Next time you're really angry with someone, write him or her a letter instead of bottling it up or lashing out. Not only will you get your point across much more clearly, but you'll also prevent yourself from getting overly worked up.

10

Today is Clean Up Your Room Day, so get rid of the clutter. Your room and your mind will be clearer.

Beauty Boost! While you're cleaning, remember to stick your pillowcases in the laundry. You should change them weekly to prevent oils from your hair from getting into your pores and causing breakouts.

11

It's Eat What You Want Day. (Really.) So go ahead . . . eat what you want! Just don't give yourself a stomachache.

While you're chowing down, rent *The Deep End of the Ocean* in honor of actor Jonathan Jackson's birthday.

12

"Sex appeal is fifty percent what you've got, and fifty percent what people think you've got."—Sophia Loren

Looking attractive is all about feeling attractive. So start your next makeover by changing your attitude.

First step: Take yourself less seriously. How? You could write a funny limerick about yourself or a friend in honor of Limerick Day.

13

Make a list of five people you admire, and then tell them—or write fan letters if you don't know them personally.

Indulge Yourself! Grab one of your friends and give each other manicures and pedicures.

May

14

Invite some friends over and have a *Star Wars*-a-thon to celebrate the birthday of George Lucas, the film's famous director.

Dare Day! While you're watching the sci-fi flicks, try an exotic fruit like star fruit, kiwi, mango, or papaya.

15

Today is National Chocolate Chip Day. Bake a batch of gooey chocolate chip cookies after school. Filling the house with that homemade smell is like aromatherapy.

Madeline Albright, the first female secretary of state, was born today in 1937.

16

Get Involved! Start a clothing or food drive at your school to help contribute to a cause you feel strongly about.

Angel star David Boreanaz has a birthday today. Rent *The Lost Boys,* David's favorite vampire flick.

17

Kick around a soccer ball with some friends in honor of soccer star Mia Hamm's birthday.

Indulge Yourself! Write a list of your favorite singers and bands and then make a mix tape with all their tunes combined.

18

"When one door closes, another opens; but we often look so long and so regretfully upon the closed door that we do not see the one which has opened for us." —Alexander Graham Bell

Feeling down about something? Focus on the positives of a bad situation.

19

Pay tribute today to those in the army, navy, marines, coast guard, and air force—it's Armed Forces Day.

20

Dare Day! Do an entire crossword puzzle by yourself—or at least give it your best effort!

21

"Happiness is a choice. You grieve, you stomp your feet, you pick yourself up and choose to be happy." —Lucy Lawless

Feeling blue? Rent a movie that always makes you laugh, even if you've seen it hundreds of times.

Then cheer someone else up. Go out for dinner and give your server an extra-big tip . . . and a smile. Today is National Waitresses/Waiters Day.

22

Astrology Alert! If you were born between today and June 21 you're a Gemini, which means you're an intellectual and a great communicator. Your perfect love matches are Aries, Aquarius, Leo, and Libra.

May

23 Singer/poet/actress Jewel was born today in 1974. Check out *Ride with the Devil,* her well-reviewed but less-seen first feature film.

---

24 In honor of Older Americans Month you could:
• Spend the day with your grandparents.
• Ask them about stories from when they were growing up.
• Visit a nursing home and talk to one of the older people who lives there.
• Send a card to your grandparents or older relatives to let them know you're thinking of them.

---

25 It's National Tap Dance Day. Try to learn a basic tap dancing step—tap, shuffle, flap. Then pop *The Miseducation of Lauryn Hill* into your CD player and groove on with some more funky dance moves. Today is the singer's birthday.

---

26 Follow these tips to get some much-needed zzz's during Better Sleep Month:
Plan to exercise for thirty minutes at least three hours before bedtime. Try using a lavender-scented eye pillow. Or pop in a nature sounds CD or tape. (You'd be surprised at how the sound of rain can knock you right out!)

27 *Friendship Tip:* Buy one of those overplayed friendship necklaces with a pal and turn it into something original—a key ring, an anklet, or maybe a couple of barrettes.

---

28 Dreaming about a juicy burger? Go for it—today is National Hamburger Day. Then ham it up with your friends and act as goofy as you want!

---

29 *Health Tip:* Get in the soy habit. Twenty-five grams of soy protein a day may reduce the risk of heart disease and some cancers. Soy can be found in tofu and all tofu products, soy milk, soy cheese, soy protein bars, edamame, and seitan. Try substituting soy milk for cow's milk with your cereal—some say it tastes even better!

---

30 Fight eating disorders. One out of every one hundred females between the ages of ten and twenty are not eating enough and should be seeing a doctor. If you think you or a friend could be at risk, talk to a trusted adult and get help.

---

31 American poet Walt Whitman was born on this day in 1819. Whitman was an original environmentalist, so plant some flowers in his honor.

May

Party of the Month: It's Barbecue Season!

Celebrate the warm weather with an evening meal outdoors and some classic summer games.

Invite: A smallish group of your closest friends.

Dress: Sundresses, or shorts and T-shirts. Whatever warm-weather clothes you've been dying to wear.

Decorations: Gingham tablecloths, colorful paper plates, Chinese lanterns, outdoor candles.

Treats: Barbecue, hot dogs, burgers, chicken, corn on the cob, baked potatoes, veggies. Macaroni and potato salad. Apple pie and ice cream.

Games/activities: Memorial Day is a time for remembrance, so get silly and play all the games you loved when you were little. Duck duck goose, red rover, musical chairs, etc.

If you're really ambitious: Set up a volleyball net and get a little tournament going.

Adopt-a-Shelter-Cat Month · Dairy Month · Turkey Lovers Month · National Iced Tea Month

Papaya Month · National Fruit and Vegetables Month

June

1 *Beauty Boost!* Get ready for summer by painting your toenails. Try sticking tiny flowers (real or fake) onto still-wet clear nail polish for a funky and fun new look.

2 It's National Rocky Road Day. Either enjoy some ice cream, or go dirt-biking . . . or both!

Party of the Month:
Casino Night!

Break out your poker face, 'cause it's time to play like the good old boys!

Invite: Twenty friends, but get three or four to help you run the games.

Dress: You and your helpers should come up with a uniform—matching vests or plastic hats or visors. Players wear what they like.

Decorations: Liven up the room with lots of red and black

to match your poker cards.

Treats: Popcorn, pretzels, chips, nuts, sodas—poker-playin' grub

Games/activities: Grab a card-playing book to learn some basic card games like poker and blackjack. Play with plastic chips or Monopoly money and have a prize for the player with the most fake dough at the end of the night.

If you're really ambitious: Scrounge up some Dixieland tunes or old-time jazz and you'll feel as if you're on a Mississippi River casino boat.

---

3 Today is Camera Day! Take a walk and bring your camera outside, snapping shots of whatever catches your eye in your neighborhood.

Friendship Tip: Set her up on a date with a cute boy. (She just might return the favor one day!)

---

4 Gear up for summer by making a list of your five favorite summer activities, the five things you'll do the day school ends, and the five things you've accomplished this year.

Indulge Yourself! Continue on with your summer preparation by watching a whole baseball game. And have some Cracker Jack while you're at it.

Actor Scott Wolf was born today in 1968.

5 "You miss one hundred percent of the shots you never take." —Wayne Gretsky

Take some risks and try something new this summer. No matter if you succeed or fail, you won't regret it.

Beauty Boost! Need an idea for something new to try? Snag fake colored streaks at your local accessory store and put them in your hair.

---

6 Today is Teacher's Day, so say thank-you to your favorite teacher (soon you won't be seeing him or her every day). And don't forget to show your appreciation for your dad—Father's Day is just around the corner! This year, why not treat him to breakfast in bed? Serve some yummy French toast.

ingredients
    6 slices of the bread of your choice
    2 eggs
    $^2/_3$ cup milk
    1 teaspoon vanilla
    2 tablespoons butter
    maple syrup

directions
1. Beat the eggs in a bowl. Stir in the milk and vanilla.
2. Heat a griddle or skillet over medium heat. Add butter to grease the pan.
3. Dip each slice of bread in egg mixture, soaking both sides. Place in pan and cook on both sides until

nicely browned.

4. Serve with maple syrup and make your dad's morning.

Makes 6 pieces of French toast

---

7 Today is National Chocolate Ice Cream Day—go for it and get an exta big cone!

---

8 Stop and smell the roses. June is National Rose Month.

Try Something New! **Grab some acrylics or pastels and paint or draw some roses while you're at it.**

---

9 "Be like a duck. Calm on the surface, but always paddling like the dickens underneath."
—actor Michael Caine

It's Donald Duck Day. (Seriously.) Allow yourself one temper tantrum in honor of the testy bird.

---

10 Rent *The Wizard of Oz*—Judy Garland (aka Dorothy) was born on this day in 1922. Pay special attention when she sings about the place where "dreams really do come true," and try to think of some ways to make your own dreams come true!

Dare Day! **Did you think of anything you could start doing know to help those dreams become reality? Then do it!**

11 "It's fun to fail sometimes because every time you get knocked down, you want to get back up and do it right." —Joshua Jackson, birthday boy

Did you tank at something recently? Try it again. You've got nothing to lose.

---

12 Actors Courteney Cox Arquette and David Arquette celebrate their wedding anniversary today. Watch any of the *Scream* movies, in which both actors star. (Cute factoid: Courteney and David met during the filming of the first movie, fell in love during the second, and got married while making the third!)

---

13 "I would urge you to be as impudent as you dare. BE BOLD, BE BOLD, BE BOLD." —writer Susan Sontag

Do something totally out there today. The bolder the better!

---

14 It's Flag Day. Salute the good ol' red, white, and blue.

Indulge Yourself! America's all about living out your dreams, so write down a list of your fantasy jobs and remember that nothing is out of your limits if you put your mind to it.

15 It's amazing what happens when you flash those pearly whites. Today is Smile Power Day.

Dare Day! Tell your boyfriend or crush how you really feel. (Remember . . . try to keep smiling!)

---

16 Bend over and touch your toes, or at least reach as close to them as you can. There—doesn't that feel good?

---

17 It's Eat Your Vegetables Day—so chomp down on some broccoli already.

Health Tip: If you have dark under-eye circles, you can heal them faster with vitamin K. Check to make sure all those veggies you're eating have enough of this important vitamim!

---

18 "Education is the most powerful weapon which you can use to change the world." —Nelson Mandela

Think back on all you've learned this year and appreciate the newer, smarter you.

---

19 "Some see things that are and ask why. I dream of things that never were and ask why not?" —Robert F. Kennedy

Have an idea you think is bizarre? Maybe it's not crazy . . . put it down on paper and share it with someone else.

20

Friendship Tip: **Know that item of clothing you never let anyone touch? Let her borrow it for a special occasion.**

21

It's the first day of summer, so go for a swim!

Some other fun ways to celebrate the season? Try grilled corn on the cob, have a picnic outside, or just enjoy the chance to model your cutest pair of shorts!

22

Astrology Alert! **If you were born between today and July 22, you're a Cancer, which means you're intuitive and love the comforts of home. Your ideal love matches are Taurus, Virgo, Scorpio, and Picses.**

It's Carson Daly's birthday. While you're hanging out at home, why don't you write down your ten fave music videos and compare your list with your friends'?

23 Wear something pink in honor of National Pink Day. And throw on R & B artist Pink's CD. By the way, do you know how Pink got her nickname? When she was seven, a boy at camp pulled down her pants in front of everyone! The singer blushed like crazy, thereby earning her the nickname Pink. Now that name sells tons of records! Have you been in an embarrassing situation lately? Why not take a tip from Pink and see if you can put a positive spin on it?

Dare Day! Clean out under your bed, then vacuum under there, too.

---

24 June is Aquarium Month, so check out the cool fishies at your local aquarium. Don't live near one? Pick up a book on marine life, or think about getting a pet goldfish!

Craft Time! Need somewhere to store your photographs? Make a decorative box. You'll need one old shoe box, craft glue, scissors, and cloth, wrapping paper, or a ton of magazine clippings. If you're using the cloth or wrapping paper, cut pieces big enough to cover the box and the lid. Then, dot glue on the top and bottom edges and the center of the piece of cloth or wrapping paper. Carefully attach cloth or wrapping paper to box, smoothing out wrinkles. For a funky alternative, use a different pattern on each side. If you're using magazine clippings, put a small amount of glue on each clipping and treat the box as if you're making a collage. Make sure you wait for everything to dry before you use the box.

25

Get your butt out of bed and watch the sunrise this morning. It's National Fruit and Vegetable Month, so while you're up early make a delish smoothie out of frozen fruit for breakfast:

ingredients

> 1 frozen banana
>
> ¹/₂ cup frozen blueberries
>
> 1 cup orange juice
>
> 1 cup plain or vanilla yogurt

directions

1. Combine banana, blueberries, orange juice, and yogurt in a blender.
2. Puree until smooth.
3. Pour into two glasses and enjoy with a friend.

26

Yum! Today is National Chocolate Pudding Day. Buy a box of Jell-O instant pudding and follow the recipe for pudding pie.

27

"Never bend your head. Always hold it high. Look the world straight in the eye."
—Helen Keller

Follow Ms. Keller's advice in honor of her birthday. Today is National Columnists' Day. Read an op-ed piece in your local paper. Who knows what you might learn.

---

28 Jean-Jacques Rousseau, the French philosopher, was born on this day in 1712. Sit down and develop a philosophy of your own—one to live by.

There's only one thing to do on actor John Cusack's birthday—rent *Say Anything*, a real American romance.

---

29 Save the Earth (and have some fun at the same time)! Recycle all of your notebooks, term papers, assignments, and tests that you don't need anymore now that school's almost over.

---

30 Bored? Start a book group with your closest friends. Each month let someone else choose the book you'll read and discuss.

Ice Cream Month.

National Baked Beans Month • National Tennis Month • Anti-Boredom Month • National

National Ice Cream Month

July

1 Ever have bubble gum ice cream? Well, today—Creative Ice Cream Flavor Day—is the day to go for it. Other suggestions? Ben & Jerry's Phish Food or Chunky Monkey.

Actress Liv Tyler has a birthday today. Rent *Armageddon* and cry with her.

---

2 *Friendship Tip:* Does your best friend have a chore to do? Volunteer to help her clean her room, weed the garden, or do the dishes. It'll get done faster and both of you can get on to doing something fun!

---

3 *Health Tip:* In honor of Stay out of the Sun Day, follow these rules about sun protection (but don't just obey them today—you should follow these rules all year long!):

• Always wear sunscreen with a minimum SPF of 15 when you're outside. If you're going swimming, make sure your lotion is waterproof. And be sure to reapply often.

• When the sun's at its peak (between the hours of nine A.M. and two P.M.), hide out in the shade. If you have to be outside, make sure to wear a hat and drink plenty of water.

• Protect your eyes by wearing sunglasses with UV protection—you'll prevent wrinkles that way, too.

• Don't forget your kisser! Keep your lips healthy by coating on a lip balm with an SPF of at least eight.

Party of the Month: Fourth of July Picnic

Hey, it's un-American to let this holiday pass without a patriotic party. Do it up right with some classic picnic fare.

Invite: About ten good friends—who can cook.

Dress: Totally casual, and bring lots of sunblock.

Decorations: Colorful picnic blankets and plastic plates and cups are all you'll need.

Treats: Potluck, baby! Everyone should bring one dish— and make sure there's enough for everyone. Assign a "course" (salad, main course, side dish, dessert, drinks) to each friend or you'll have ten plates of brownies. Not that that's necessarily a bad thing.

Games/Activities: Outdoor games like Frisbee, Kadima, baseball, badminton, and good old-fashioned catch.

If you're really ambitious: Find out where your local fireworks display is being held and get there early in the day to snag a prime viewing spot.

4 Independence Day! Spend the day on you, you, you—and don't waste one second worrying about what anyone else thinks.

5 Take a trip to the circus in honor of P. T. Barnum. The founder of Barnum & Bailey Circus was born on this day in 1810. Or just dress up like a clown and teach your dog some stupid tricks.

6 It's National Fried Chicken Day—make an outing to your local KFC!
It's Sylvester Stallone's birthday. Honor Rocky by renting *Boxing Fitness for Women* and learn how to spar like a champ. It'll help you work off that fried chicken, too!

7 Sit down with one of your parents and ask him or her to teach you how to balance a checkbook. Once you've become a budgeting whiz, celebrate with something seriously sweet and fruity. It's National Strawberry Sundae Day!

8 Today is Video Games Day. Play *Pokémon* all day long, guilt free!

9 *Health Tip:* Feel tired all the time? Well, now that it's summer, maybe you're getting too much sleep. Try setting your alarm a few times a week and get a jump on the day.

July

10 *Beauty Boost!* All that swimming and time in the sun have your hair looking less than healthy? Go to the drugstore and look for shampoos and conditioners with vitamin B5, which can help strengthen your strands. You can also try a leave-in conditioner that'll keep working on your hair all day long.

---

11 Bored with summer? Why not return to your roots? Strap on a pair of comfy hiking shoes and hightail it to the nearest state park for a long hike and some quality time with Mother Nature. Don't forget to be safe, of course! Bring a buddy and make sure to follow the marked trails. Want information on parks near you? Check out Great Outdoor Recreation Pages http://www.gorp.com or visit the National Parks Conservation Association at http://www.npca.org.

---

12 National Pecan Pie Day—treat yourself to a warm slice . . . with a scoop of vanilla ice cream on top.

That '70s Show's Topher Grace was born today in 1978. Celebrate by pulling on a pair of bell-bottoms and scoring a lava lamp at a novelty store.

---

13 Rent the entire *Indiana Jones* trilogy in honor of Harrison Ford's birthday. Hum the theme song wherever you go!

14 *Get Involved!* Do something for the community on National Cheer Up the Lonely Day. Help out at a nursing home and spend some time with the residents there. Or you could even call a friend who's been feeling blue, and let her know you're there. You'll brighten someone's day (not to mention your own)!

---

15 It's Respect Canada Day. Play some hockey, use real maple syrup on your pancakes, and listen to Alanis Morissette.

Not sure what to do to show your respect for actor Scott Foley's birthday? Munch a bunch of Mrs. Fields cookies. (We know—such a painful sacrifice!) Scott worked there while he was trying to break into the biz.

---

16 *Craft Time!* Make a cool frame for your favorite picture of you and your friends. You'll need a plain wooden or plastic frame from a dollar store, some funky rhinestones, and glue. Use the rhinestones to decorate the frame, dotting them with a tiny bit of glue to attach them. Make sure you try out some color schemes and patterns before you glue them down. Cool alternatives to rhinestones include glitter, funky old buttons, bottle caps, pennies, and beads.

Friendship Tip: Make some more frames to give your friends for their photos of you together. You can use a common theme or color so that the frames match each others!

17 "It's not going to kill me if I never get a gold. How can you say that six minutes at the Olympics should decide whether you have a happy life?"
—Olympic silver medalist Michelle Kwan.

If Michelle can be that laid-back about the oldest, most prestigious contest in the world, maybe you should let your last loss go. You'll come out a winner in the end.

---

18 *Indulge Yourself!* Have a hot fudge sundae on National Ice Cream Day. Or, if you prefer upscale goodies, be outrageous and extravagant and taste some caviar in honor of National Caviar Day.

Pick up *Peacemakers: Winners of the Nobel Peace Prize* to find out what birthday boy Nelson Mandela and many others have done to make our world a better place.

---

19 *Dare Day!* Do you tune out when your friends start talking about baseball? Grab a copy of Baseball for Dummies and find out what they're talking about when they start spouting "RBIs" and "ERAs."

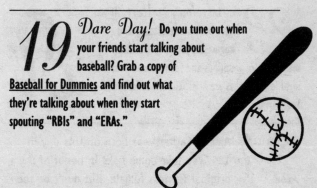

20 On this day in 1969, Neil Armstrong was strolling on the moon. Why not grab a comfy blanket and a few friends and lie out under the moon and stars? It's even more relaxing (and less wrinkle-inducing) than lying out in the sun. Don't be afraid to let your mind wander, too—if Neil could go to the moon, then you shouldn't limit yourself!

---

21 Today is National Tug-of-War Tournament Day. Round up some pals, divide up into two teams, and see who wins!

Actor Josh Hartnett of *The Faculty* celebrates his birthday today.

---

22 Weather too hot for ya? Make some paper snowflakes and decorate your windows with them, then visit one of those year-round Christmas shops. You'll be chillin' in no time.

---

23 *Astrology Alert!* If you were born between today and August 22, you're a Leo, which means you're ambitious and spontaneous. Your ideal love matches are Aries, Libra, Gemini, and Sagittarius.

---

24 Amelia Earhart was born on this day in 1897, so take some risks in honor of the original fearless female. But don't be too

risky. You don't want to face the same sad fate she did.

Big day for birthdays! Both actress/singer Jennifer Lopez and Oscar-winner Anna Paquin were born today.

---

25 Grab a friend and head for the tennis court. It's National Tennis Month!

"How you doin'?" *Friends'* Matt LeBlanc's doing pretty well—it's his birthday.

---

26 It's All or Nothing Day, so go for it! Finish a task you've been procrastinating about, tell someone you love them, or push it to the limit on your morning run. You've got nothing to lose!

Indulge Yourself: After you've accomplished your big feat, take an extra long soak in the tub until you get those cool prune fingers.. Remember it is All or Nothing Day!

---

27 The Internet isn't just for shopping, you know! Why not check out the official sites—and sights—of some foreign countries. Tour Europe from the comfort of your own home! Here are a few websites to get you started:

- http://www.ireland.travel.ie (Ireland)
- http://www.abserv.co.at/abserv/tourist/ (Austria)
- http://www.itwg.com (Italy)

28 It's National Milk Chocolate Day, and chocolate is a good source for cancer-fighting antioxidants. So crack open your favorite Hershey Bar! Then pop *Willy Wonka and the Chocolate Factory* in your VCR and sing along with the Oompa Loompas.

---

29 Miss your friends from school? Gather up a bunch of photos, concert and movie ticket stubs, school spirit paraphernalia, and whatever else reminds you of your buds and make a funky friendship collage. While you're at it, why not make one for your best friend, too?

---

30 *Friends* actress Lisa Kudrow and comedian Tom Green (*Road Trip*) were born this day in 1963 and 1971, respectively. What a great reason to act as silly as possible today! How about singing in the shower—loudly—even if everyone in your family is home? You know Phoebe would. And you really know Tom would. (But he'd probably do something gross, too!)

---

31 Today is Parents' Day, so why not try doing something thoughtful for your mom and dad?

Don't have any ideas? You could:
• Offer to baby-sit your younger sibling so they can have the day off.
• Clean up the house.

• Make them dinner—and do the dishes afterward! Try out this Penne, tomato, and mozzarella salad for something tasty and easy:

Ingredients:

1 16–ounce package penne pasta
$\frac{1}{4}$ cup olive oil
1 bunch scallions, chopped
1 garlic clove, minced
pinch of salt and pepper
8 ounces cherry tomatoes, cut into halves
6 ounces mozzarella cheese, diced
$\frac{1}{2}$ cup grated Parmesan cheese
1 bunch fresh basil leaves

Directions:

1. Cook penne in a large pot of boiling salted water as directed on package. Drain.
2. Heat olive oil in a small saucepan. Add the scallions and cook, stirring occasionally for two to three minutes.
3. Add the garlic and cook for a couple more minutes.
4. Add the cooked pasta, salt, and pepper to the pan.
5. Turn the heat down low, add the tomatoes, and stir. Then add the cheeses and stir.
6. Turn heat off. Tear basil leaves in half and add to pasta.
7. Serve to your parents and watch their jaws drop!

Makes 6 servings.

August

1 *It's Friendship Day*—time to call everyone you've neglected on your summer vacation.

2 Today is National Ice-Cream Sandwich Day. Take two chocolate chip cookies and the ice cream of your choice and make your own.

Dare Day! Listen to a CD you'd never consider—all the way through—and try to appreciate the appeal. (Maybe the ice-cream sandwich will help it go down easier!)

3 What's summer without watermelon? Have a big juicy slice today— National Watermelon Day.

It's also National Golf Month, so you could head to your nearest mini-golf course or driving range. Just wash your sticky watermelon fingers before you grab the nine iron, would ya?

4 Are you a twin? Know any? Today is Twins' Day Festival.

Some famous twins:
Jason and Jeremy London (*Dazed and Confused, Party of Five*)
Brittany and Cynthia Daniel (*Sweet Valley High, Dawson's Creek*)

August

Tia and Tamara Mowry (*Sister, Sister*)
Brandon and Brenda Walsh (*Beverly Hills, 90210,* played
by Jason Priestley and Shannen Doherty)

---

5 It's National Mustard Day! Invite some pals over for hot dogs and load on the French's or Gulden's.

Try Something New! See how long you and your friends can talk without using the word "like." You'll be laughing in no time!

---

6 Check out a sign language book from the library and teach yourself the signing alphabet. Then show a few friends how to spell their names.

---

7 *Beauty Boost!* (And a *Health Tip*) Want some buff abs for that bikini? Crunches are always good but so is . . . belly dancing! Spend 20 minutes dancing in your room and make sure to move those hips and twist that stomach. You'd be surprised how good those ab muscles feel!

---

8 Today is Family Day. Make a point of spending the day with yours. Need some ideas for activities? Go to the zoo, hit a local park and play basketball, or just whip out that Pictionary game and find out if your 'rents have any artistic ability.

It's a boy band birthday bonanza. Drew Lachey of 98° and J. C. Chasez of 'N Sync were both born on this day in 1976.

Party of the Month: *Latin Fiesta*

Live *la vida loca* with a little Latin music, spicy food, and a lot of good, loud fun to wrap up the summer.

Invite: A big crowd of guys and girls who are not afraid to dance.

Dress: Comfy, colorful clothes you can move in.

Decorations: Bright, colorful streamers and balloons, strings of twinkling lights.

Treats: Chips, salsa, guacamole, chili, tacos and burritos, sodas and citrusy drinks.

Games/activities: Get a video that teaches basic steps and learn to salsa, merengue, and more. Have a dance-off and see who was made to mambo!

If you're really ambitious: Have a basic Spanish book handy and make sure each of your friends learns to say five useful things in Spanish. Then you can teach one another what you've learned.

9 National Polka Festival. That's all we have to say about that.

10 Sleep late. Be a couch potato. Put it off till tomorrow. After all, today is Lazy Day.
While you're at it, why not make a list of five relaxing things to do—and try to keep "watching TV" out of it.

11 It's American Artists Appreciation month. Head to a museum to study the works up close, or if you're feeling ambitious, become an artist yourself! Whip out some paints, clay, or whatever moves you, and get creative.

12 Have a Jan Brady complex? Well, today— Middle Child's Day—is your day. Let everyone know and bask in the attention!
Birthday boy Casey Affleck's not a middle child, but he is a younger brother. Rent *Good Will Hunting* and laugh at his sibling rivalry with Ben. (The big bro celebrates his birthday three days from today.)

13 Filmmaker Alfred Hitchcock was born on this day in 1899. Rent *Rear Window* with a friend. Not only is it suspenseful and spooky, but you can take some grace tips from Grace Kelly—the picture of sophisticated beauty.

Sick of sitting around? While you're at the video store, pick up an exercise tape and you and your bud can get active.

---

14 You know crystals look cool, but did you know some people think they have special powers? If you're willing to try them out, check out what these crystals can do for you:

Carnelian relieves PMS and helps you chill.

Rose quartz is all about love and can help heal a broken heart.

Amethyst will help you concentrate.

Hematite gives you happy vibes.

---

15 Take some time for yourself in honor of Relaxation Day. Light a few scented candles, change into your comfiest clothes, and play some relaxing music.

Speaking of music, maybe dancing is what mellows your mood. Groove to some Janis Joplin and Jimi Hendrix. The original Woodstock began today in 1969.

16 Invite some friends over and have a retro-80s Madonna fest for her birthday—dance to her first two CDs, *Madonna* and *Like A Virgin*, wear plenty of lace and neon, and watch *Desperately Seeking Susan*.

---

17 Today is National Thrift Shop Day. Clean your closet of those clothes you haven't worn in years and drop them off at your local thrift shop. While you're there, shop around. You never know what gem you might find!

Health Tip: Help your teeth and skin by swearing off soda for a week and drinking water in its place. Then see if you can keep it up!

---

18 Bad Poetry Day. Challenge your buds to write some really bad rhymes, then whip up some latte and have a dramatic reading. It's sure to generate some laughs.

---

19 "I give every French fry a fair chance." —Cameron Diaz.

How do you like your potatoes? Fried, baked, or mashed? Make like Cameron and enjoy every one. Have 'em any way you want—today is Potato Day!

Bill Clinton and *Friends* star Matthew Perry both celebrate birthdays today. Interesting pair, no?

20

Today is Radio Day. Tune in to National Public Radio and learn something new.

Dare Day! Okay, we know NPR can get serious, so have a little fun and climb a tree. You know you want to.

21

Want to get in touch with your spiritual center? Meditation is good for the soul. Turn out all the lights in your room, light a scented candle, and chill out with a CD made to mellow, like *Yoga Zone: Music for Meditation*.

22

Today is Be an Angel Day. Perform a random act of kindness. Or you could pretend to be a vampire. Just kidding.

23

Astrology Alert! If you were born between today and September 22, you're a Virgo, which means you're cheerful and witty. Your ideal love matches are Scorpio, Cancer, Capricorn, and Taurus.

24 Long day with nothing to do? Make yourself a mix tape of all your favorite summer songs, then pop it in your Walkman, take it to the town pool or local park, and lie out. (Don't forget the sunscreen!) When you get too hot, come home and cool off with a creamy milk shake. They're easy to make!

ingredients
- 1 cup milk
- 1 scoop ice cream of your choice
- 2 tablespoons chocolate (or other flavor) syrup

directions
1. Add all the ingredients into a blender and blend until combined.
2. Pour into a glass and enjoy!

Makes one milk shake

---

25 C'mon, get over it already! That's right, it's Kiss and Make Up Day. Forgive a friend, let your brother borrow that Game Boy, and stop fighting with your mom. You'll feel 100 percent better!

"Is that your final answer?" Regis Philbin, the host of *Who Wants to Be a Millionaire?*, has a birthday today. Try playing along on-line at www.abc.com.

26 It's Women's Equality Day. Bond with your mom and your sisters over a tall glass of lemonade.

---

27 Mother Teresa was born on this day in 1910. Let her spirit live on by devoting some of your time to others—sign up to volunteer at a soup kitchen or enroll in a big sister program.

Friendship Tip: Be generous with someone closer to home. Rather get a head-to-toe sunburn than see that flick your bud wants to see? Go anyway and keep her company. That's what friends are for.

---

28 "I don't think of myself as a teen, I think of myself as a businesswoman."
—Ambitious singer LeAnn Rimes was born on this day in 1982.

Indulge Yourself! We don't all have to be businesswomen. Buy a funky PEZ dispenser and a big bag of the sugar candies in your favorite flavor.

---

29 "Don't compromise yourself. You're all you've got."—Janis Joplin
If you're having a hard time sticking to your beliefs, just remember they're what make you you.

30 Celebrate National Toasted Marshmallow Day. Ask your parents to help you light up the grill and get toasty!

31 Up your cosmic sense. Check out a book on palm reading from the library, then tell all your friends their fortunes.

Self-Improvement Month • Cable TV Month • National Chicken Month • National Courtesy Month •

Rice Month • Classical Music Month • Self-Improvement Month • International Square •

September

1

Ben or Noel? Ben. Scott Speedman was born today in 1975. Go for a last summer swim—Scott once considered swimming in the Olympics.

Party of the Month: Back to School Bash

You've had a long summer away from school and it's time to get reacquainted with all your friends—before you're tossed to the teachers and books.

Invite: 15 friends. And make sure you get together anyone you meant to keep in touch with but didn't.

Dress: Casual and comfy. Jeans and T-shirts.

Decorations: You're going out this time! Everyone should gather at the local bowling alley, pizza place, or roller rink. Someplace fun.

Treats: Wherever you end up,

bring your own homemade dessert—cookies, cupcakes, or muffins—to add your own touch.

Games/activities: If you're bowling, assign teams and have a competition. Make sure everyone shares at least one cool story from the summer vacation—just like your teachers made you do when you were little.

If you're really ambitious: Have each of your guests bring a blank notebook they'll be using for school, and have everyone sign the covers. This way, when you're sitting in class, dreaming of summer, you can remember your final summer fling!

---

2 *Indulge Yourself!* Spend a half hour in front of the mirror trying on different hairstyles. Then check out the slick do's in <u>The Matrix</u>—it's star Keanu Reeves's birthday!

---

3 *Friendship Tip:* Hit the beauty counter at the mall with a friend and get makeovers together. Nothing like a new look to start the new school year!

---

4 Bring that person who delivers your paper every morning a bagel. Today is Newspaper Carrier Day. Then why don't you try reading the newspaper cover to cover? Or at least the comic strips!

---

5 Don't rush—today is Be Late for Something Day. Unless, of course, it's the first day of school. Then it's Be on Time if Not Early for Something Day!

6 Don't put off tomorrow . . . Today is Fight Procrastination Day. (Ironic, considering yesterday was Be Late for Something Day—maybe you can get done today whatever you didn't get around to yesterday!)

---

7 Buy a bunch of oranges and squeeze your own OJ.

---

8 It's Classical Music Month. Head to your nearest CD store and listen to some stuff from the classical section. Ask the salesperson if you don't know where to start, and splurge on your favorite disc. You'll feel so cultured!

---

9 Today is Teddy Bear Day. Hug your furry old friend.

Reese Witherspoon and Ryan Phillippe's baby girl, Ava Elizabeth, celebrates her birthday today. Wonder how many teddy bears she has?

Dawson's Creek actress Michelle Williams was born on this day in 1980.

10 Bring up an issue with some friends and see what everyone's take on it is in honor of Swap Ideas Day.

While you're swapping ideas, why not exchange clothes, too? You'll both get a new look without dropping any cash.

---

11 *Dare Day!* Be extra nice to your brother or sister. Might have some interesting results . . .

---

12 Today is National Grandparents' Day. Give 'em a call and let them know what you've been up to.

---

13 Walk under a ladder, let a black cat cross your path, and knock on plastic in honor of Defy Superstition Day.

---

14 "Test scores do not determine what you will be when you grow up. Rather, hard work and material learned do."
—NASA member Jennifer Kwong

Don't stress if you didn't do as well as you hoped on a test. Just keep studying hard. It's what you learn that's important.

Indulge Yourself! Celebrate National Cream-Filled Doughnut Day by munching some Krispy Kreme or Dunkin' Donuts . . . guilt-free.

15 Have you ever imagined where you'll be ten years from today? Try it—and be as outrageous as you can.

16 Slap some honey on a piece of toast in honor of National Honey Month— and give your honey an extra kiss!

17 Grab a book and a computer and learn HTML. Then you'll be able to create your own website in honor of your favorite star, your school, your dog . . . whatever!

18 It's National Play-Doh Day. Pick up some of the colorful clay and regress . . . you'll love it.

19 Rebecca Romijn-Stamos married John Stamos on this day in 1998. Pop some dance music into your stereo and put on an impromptu fashion show in honor of MTV's *House of Style* hostess.

Dare Day! Now that you're in the style zone, paint a wall in your room a different color (but make sure you ask your parents first!).

20 Today is National Punch Day. We're not sure if this is the physical kind or the fruity kind, but we prefer the fruity.

21 Do like Oprah and make a list of ten things you're grateful for in honor of World Gratitude Day.

Going back to school isn't on your list? Invite some pals over and get over the back-to-school blues by making some banana splits in honor of International Banana Day!

ingredients

    4 bananas
    2 pints of the ice cream of your choice
    chocolate syrup or chocolate fudge sauce
    whipped cream
    chopped nuts

directions

1. Slice the bananas in half lengthwise. Place two halves each in four different bowls.
2. Place three scoops of ice cream in between the banana halves.
3. Drizzle syrup or fudge on top of ice cream and bananas.
4. Spray whipped cream on top.
5. Sprinkle nuts on top.

Makes 4 banana splits

22

"It's the good girls who keep the diaries; the bad girls never have the time."
— Tallulah Bankhead

Haven't written in your journal in a while? Be a "good girl" and get back to it today—Dear Diary Day. Don't have a diary? Now's the perfect time to start one. Fill it with your thoughts, dreams, doodles, letters to yourself, or whatever comes to your brain.

23

Astrology Alert! If you were born between today and October 23, you're a Libra, which means you're easygoing and kind. Your ideal love matches are Leo, Gemini, Sagittarius, and Aquarius.

24

Want some new accessories for fall, but already spent all your cash on clothes? Go to your favorite accessory store and check out some of the beaded necklaces and bracelets. Remember the color scheme of your favorite, then head to a craft store and pick up beads and elastic at a fraction of the cost. You can make jewelry for yourself and your friends!

25

Today is National Comic Book Day. Grab a copy of your favorite comic and kick back. Then dress up in some hip-hop duds and get jiggy wit' it—it's Will Smith's birthday.

26 Smile at the people next door—Today is National Good Neighbor Day.
Even better—bring them some pancakes to celebrate National Pancake Day at the same time!

---

27 Don't let school stress get you down. If you need a good way to relieve aggression, scream as loud as you can into a pillow. It's a lot less damaging than taking it out on a friend or family member.

---

28 Make this year different than the rest. Get involved in a new club, committee, or extracurricular activity in school. We bet birthday girl Gwyneth Paltrow was in the drama club!

---

29 *Indulge Yourself!* Play that top forty song you love over and over until you drive the neighbors nuts. (After all—National Good Neighbor Day is over!)

---

30 It's the first day of fall, so go appreciate the changing leaves. Try rolling around in a pile of them like you did when you were little, when no one's watching.

Computer Learning Month • National Apple Jack Month • National Clock Month • National Dessert Month

National Seafood Month • National Kitchen and Bath Month •

Vegetarian Awareness Month • Computer Learning Month • National Apple Jack Month • National

October

Clock Month • National Dessert Month • Adopt-A-

1 Cook up some yummy acorn squash in honor of World Vegetarian Day. This autumn veggie is so sweet you'll think it's dessert!

ingredients

- 1 acorn squash
- 1 tablespoon butter
- 2 tablespoons brown sugar or maple syrup

directions

1. Preheat the oven to 350°F.
2. With a sharp knife, carefully cut the squash in half.
3. With a spoon, scoop the seeds out.
4. Place both halves of the squash, skin side down, on a cookie sheet. Spoon butter and brown sugar or maple syrup onto both halves.
5. Place squash in the oven and bake for about an hour.
6. Take squash out and serve.

Makes 2–4 servings

---

2 "An eye for an eye makes the whole world blind."
—Mohandas Gandhi
Indian leader, philosopher, and pacifist Mohandas Gandhi was born on this day in 1869.

---

3 October is Breast Cancer Awareness Month. Pick up a pamphlet at your doctor's office and find out how to protect yourself.
Singers Gwen Stefani and Backstreet Boy Kevin

Richardson celebrate their birthdays today. Sing your lungs out to No Doubt, then mellow out with some slow BSB tunes.

---

4 It's party day in Hollywood! Rachael Leigh Cook and Alicia Silverstone were both born today. Rent *She's All That* and *Clueless,* then give yourself a makeover. You'll definitely be inspired.

---

5 Lie down on your back, close your eyes, and listen to your heart beat. You'll be surprised at how relaxing it is!

---

6 Eat a frankfurter and throw some sauerkraut on it. Today is German-American Day.

Dare Day! Pick a stock, pretend you invested 100 bucks in it, and monitor it for the next month in the paper or even on-line.

---

7 *Craft Time!* Freshen up your room with some homemade potpourri. You'll need two cups of rose petals, a tablespoon of cloves, a tablespoon of nutmeg, a tablespoon of cinnamon, and a half cup of brown sugar. Lay the rose petals out on a paper towel and let them dry for a week. Once the petals are dried out, mix all the ingredients together and place them in a pretty bowl or jar.

Friendship Tip: If she does something embarrassing, tell her it's okay instead of laughing at her.

8 The talented Mr. Matt Damon was born today in 1970. Rent *School Ties*, one of his early movies, and enjoy all the eye candy—Brendan Fraser, Ben Affleck, Chris O'Donnell, and Anthony Rapp costarred with Matt.

9 October is Computer Learning Month. Set a new computer goal for yourself. You can already do it all? Devote some time to teaching your parent or a computer-clueless friend the basics. And be patient!

10 Today is Angel Food Cake Day. Have a slice with some strawberries . . . it is low-fat.

11 "When you get to the end of your rope, tie a knot in it and hang on."
—Eleanor Roosevelt
A woman ahead of her time, Ms. Roosevelt was born on this day in 1884. Feel as if you're under too much pressure? You don't have to face it alone—talk to an adult you trust.

12 Believe it or not, today is International Moment of Frustration Scream Day. So go ahead, let it out. Just try not to break any glass with your yelling.

13 *Friendship Tip:* Is your BFF having trouble in a certain class? Offer to do your homework with her and then you'll both have someone there to help if you have any questions.

---

14 It's National Dessert Day. Have the delish sweet of your choice.

American poet e. e. cummings was born on this day in 1894. The writer rarely used capital letters in his poems, so try writing one of your own, and pay no attention to minor details.

---

15 October is Vegetarian Awareness Month. Why not try subbing some veggie dishes for your regular meat ones once in a while, like a grilled veggie burger instead of a hamburger?

---

16 It's Dictionary Day, a perfect time to start a great new hobby. Get some friends together to play this fun word game. Pick a random weird word out of the dictionary and write down the definition on a scrap of paper. Then tell your friends what the word is and have them write down their own made-up definitions. Collect the papers and read all the definitions out loud. All your friends have to try to guess which meaning is the real one. Let another friend pick the next word and so on. Once everyone has had a chance, whoever has guessed the most correct definitions wins!

17 Today is Gaudy Day. Tell all your friends to wear the tackiest getups they can find, and you do the same. Bring your camera along with you and snap shots of your crazy outfits.

It's Chris Kirkpatrick of 'N Sync's birthday.

18 "The important thing is not to stop questioning." —Albert Einstein

Speak up in class. If you're confused, ask a question.

19 You don't have to spend all day today—Evaluate Your Life Day—in deep contemplation. Just make a list of all the things you like about your daily existence. Then make a list of five things you'd like to change—and how you'll go about doing it.

20 "Family faces are magic mirrors. Looking at people who belong to us, we see the past, present, and future. We make discoveries about ourselves." —writer Gail Lumet Buckley

Don't take your family for granted; they're the best support system you have.

21 *Dare Day!* Bike a mile and make sure there are a lot of hills in your route.

Indulge Yourself! Play with some liquid bubbles once the homework's done.

October

22 It's National Nut Day. Eat one, or act like one . . . or both!

---

23 Today is National Mole Day. Take a brown eyeliner pencil and draw a Cindy Crawford–like beauty mark wherever you'd like—just for the fun of it.

---

24 *Astrology Alert!* If you were born between today and November 22, you're a Scorpio, which means you're magnetic and have a passionate nature. Your perfect love matches are Pisces, Capricorn, Cancer, and Virgo.

---

25 Go pumpkin picking with a bunch of friends. Whoever picks the best pumpkin wins a little prize.

---

26 *Indulge Yourself!* Window-shop on the Web. Okay, and maybe buy something, too. But get your parent's permission first.

---

27 *Beauty Boost!* In a large basin, combine warm water, some baby oil, and the juice from one lemon. Soak your feet for 15 minutes. Then, take a pumice stone and gently work it over calluses . Finish off the royal foot treatment by rubbing moisturizer on the bottom of your feet.

Party of the Month: A Haunting Halloween

It's time to dress up and get freaky, but don't be a bum about it. Come up with a theme for your scary soiree. Have your friends dress up as their favorite characters, famous couples, or as deathly monsters only.

Invite: A crowd of creative, costumed friends.

Dress: We think you've gotten that point already.

Decorations: Go all out with orange and black from crepe paper to balloons to tableware to everything! And grab some of those fake cobwebs, too. Heck, just raid your local party store, and get one of those spooky sounds tapes to freak out your friends as they come to the door.

October

Treats: Candy, candy, candy! And apple cider, of course.

Games/activities: Classic costume contest, pumpkin carving, bobbing for apples.

If you're really ambitious: Rent *The Rocky Horror Picture Show* and learn to do the Time Warp!

---

28 "I now understand, at long last, that in a great relationship you can still maintain all the things that make you happy. I think a lot of my misunderstanding of relationships was in thinking I had to evaporate to be someone's girlfriend."
—Julia Roberts, birthday girl

If you have a boyfriend, make sure that you're not losing yourself in the relationship. Have you given up anything you truly love for him? Get it back.

---

29 *Indulge Yourself!* It's Hermit Day. Take some time for you instead of putting everyone else first.

---

30 Eat as much candy corn as you want on National Candy Corn Day . . . without getting sick. Then, in the spirit of Halloween tomorrow, sit down and make a list of three things that scare you. Try to face at least one of those fears.

---

31 Halloween! You're never too old to go trick-or-treating!

International Drum Month • American

American Indian Heritage Month • Great American Smokeout Month • Stamp Collecting Month

Month • International Drum Month

November

1 The first women's medical school opened on this day in 1848. (Paying attention in science could pay off!)

Indulge Yourself! Have a Hacky Sack tournament with a bunch of pals after school.

---

2 Make a list of your five favorite characters from TV, movies, or books. Then sit down and try to figure out what qualities you love about them.

---

3 Today is Sandwich Day. Make sure you chow down on one of your favorite kinds for lunch.

---

4 Make use of those great autumn apples by making a scrumptious apple crisp.

ingredients

- 4 apples, peeled, cored, and sliced
- $\frac{1}{2}$ cup raisins
- $\frac{1}{2}$ cup brown sugar
- $\frac{3}{4}$ cup sugar
- 1 cup all-purpose flour
- 1 teaspoon ground cinnamon
- $\frac{1}{4}$ teaspoon salt
- 1 egg
- 2 tablespoons butter, melted

November

directions

1. Preheat oven to 375°F.
2. In a 8 x 8 or 9 x 9 square baking pan, mix together sliced apples and raisins with brown sugar.
3. In a separate bowl, mix together flour, sugar, cinnamon, and salt.
4. In another small bowl, beat egg, then mix in the melted butter. Stir egg-butter mixture into flour mixture. Spread this mixture evenly over apples and raisins.
5. Bake for 30 to 40 minutes, or until the topping is golden and crisp.

Makes approximately 12 servings

---

5 *Craft Time* Why not make some chopsticks to hold your hair back for a new look? You'll need two plain wooden chopsticks, colorful high-gloss paints, paintbrushes, glue, and rhinestones. Paint the chopsticks. Let the paint dry. Add a second coat if too much wood is showing through. With a tiny bit of glue, attach the rhinestones to the thicker end of the chopstick. Let dry, and wear!

---

6 Today is Saxophone Day. So snag a jazz CD and hear how sexy that sax can sound!

---

7 Polish chemist/physicist Marie Curie was born on this day in 1867. In honor of this feminist trail-blazer, work a little harder on your science homework or volunteer to do an extra credit experiment.

8 Can't think of a subject for that short story or poem? Why not write about yourself? Show the world how cool you are!

9 Surf the Web and do some research on the Berlin Wall—it came down on this day in 1989.
     Hottie Nick Lachey of 98° celebrates his birthday today.

10 *Dare Day!* Sit with a new crowd in the cafeteria today.

11 Today is Veterans Day. Are any of your family members veterans? Maybe you could ask them if they have any stories they'd like to share with you.

Get Involved! Emulate actor Leonardo DiCaprio, who was born today in 1974, by working for the environment—it's the cause Leo feels most strongly about.

12 It's National Pizza with the Works Day. Grab a slice after school—just make sure it's not too heavy to lift!

Between the ages of 11 and 18, your body has an increased need for iron. Remember to eat plenty of meat, poultry, fish, leafy green vegetables, rice, and beans—all great sources of iron. You could get a good start by loading up that pizza slice with meat or spinach!

13

"I've learned to take time for myself and to treat myself with a great deal of love and a great deal of respect. 'Cause I like me . . . I think I'm pretty cool." —Whoopi Goldberg

Actress/comedienne Whoopi Goldberg celebrates her birthday today.

14

Go to the library and check out a book of impressionist paintings. Claude Monet, the most famous of the French impressionists, was born on this day in 1840.

Indulge Yourself! Since you're drinking in all that culture, you might as well let yourself drink all the soda you want today.

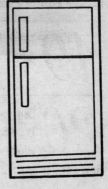

15

It's National Clean Out Your Refrigerator Day. Don't even try to figure out what that growing green stuff is—just chuck it.

16 You know that person at school you just can't stand? Well, suck it up and be civil today, the Day for Tolerance.

17 Do your best catwalk in honor of RuPaul for the diva's birthday.

Try Something New! Grab a bunch of friends and go ice-skating.

18 *Craft Time!* Be a help to your family by making these pretty place cards in preparation for Thanksgiving. You'll need brown, orange, and yellow construction paper; white paint marker; black marker; Scotch tape; scissors; glue; and leaves you collect from outside. Cut the paper into strips and write your guests' names in the center of the strips. Use the white marker for the brown paper and the black marker for the orange and yellow paper. Making a circle, attach the two ends of each strip and tape them together. Delicately glue leaves to the inside of the ring, just behind the guest's name. Bravo! You've just made a colorful accessory for your Thanksgiving table.

19 Today is Have a Bad Day Day. So let it all out.

20 Can you believe they have a day for this? It's Absurdity Day, a chance to say whatever silly thoughts come to your brain. How cool!

November

Dare Day! Give yourself a theme song—remember to make it as absurd as you want.

---

21 Today is World Hello Day. Why don't you try learning how to say hello and good-bye in four different languages?

---

22 *Dare Day!* Paint each fingernail and toenail a different color.

---

23 *Astrology Alert!* If you were born between today and December 21, you're a Sagittarius, which means you're adventurous and optimistic. Your perfect love matches are Libra, Aquarius, Leo, and Aries.

---

24 Express your girl power by writing a list of ten reasons you're happy to be a girl. Then make a list of the top ten women you admire. What could you do to be like them?

Roswell's Katherine Heigl was born today in 1978. Rent *My Father, the Hero,* one of Katherine's early movies, to find out why she's a woman worth looking up to.

---

25 *Indulge Yourself!* Flip through some wedding magazines and fantasize about your walk down the aisle.

26 Feeling broke? Don't stress out over what to get your friends. This is a time for fun, not financial ruin! Suggest a grab bag for you and your friends, so you'll each only have to buy one gift instead of ten. And set a price limit, like five or ten dollars. You'd be amazed at how much more fun gifts can be when you have to put a little creative thought into them!

---

27 Try out some martial arts moves, or sign up for a self-defense class. Bruce Lee, the Chinese martial arts master, was born on this day in 1940.

If you don't have one of your own, listen to one of your parents' Jimi Hendrix CDs. The legendary guitarist was born on this day in 1942.

---

28 *Health Tip:* Bonding with your pets is said to lower stress and blood pressure. So hang with Fido for an hour today and thank him for your mood boost with a nice Milk-Bone.

---

29 It's Square Dance Day. Grab a partner and do-si-do!

---

30 Mark Twain was born on this day in 1835. Read one of the author's lesser known but amazing short stories, "The Mysterious Stranger."

November

Party of the Month: Totally Eighties

Two decades ago we were living in a material world where a Duran Duran ticket was as hot as a double bill of 'N Sync and the Backstreet Boys. It's time to celebrate pop history.

Invite: A plethora of partyers.

Dress: Cheese it up '80s style with leg warmers and off-the-shoulder shirts in fluorescents and black. Stock up on black rubber bracelets, rhinestones, lace stockings, and glitter gloves.

Decorations: The eighties were all about glitz and glamour. Go for sparkly decorations, flashing lights, and a disco ball.

Treats: Coke and Pepsi (the eighties were the cola war years), lots of greasy junk food, but also some fresh veggies and dip.

Games/activities: Rent the classics—*Sixteen Candles, The Breakfast Club, Flashdance.* Snag the '80s version of Trivial Pursuit and test your knowledge.

If you're really ambitious: Find some '80s dance tunes from Janet Jackson, Madonna, Michael Jackson, etc., and do a little break dancing.

December

1 Today is Eat a Red Apple Day. So keep that doctor away!

It's also World AIDS Day. Try to find out if there are any rallies or walks near you and show your support.

---

2 Christmas, Hanukkah, and Kwanzaa are all this month. Need some ideas for special gifts for your family that won't break the bank? Why not make your own unique present to show how much you care? You could . . . make a mix tape for your family member comprised of all their favorite tunes, write a poem or a short story, make a piece of artwork (a drawing, painting, sculpture, or photograph), or even make coupons good for things like a free hour of baby-sitting, a home-made ice-cream sundae, or breakfast in bed.

---

3 Whether or not you celebrate Hanukkah, learn how to play dreidel—it's a lot of fun! Do you know why Hanukkah lasts eight days? It's because the oil that was supposed to light the temple for only one day miraculously lasted for eight!

4 *Health Tip:* You're about to go on an eating fest with all the holidays, so try one of these healthy and yummy snacks: ice-cream sandwiches made with frozen yogurt and oatmeal cookies, peanut butter with apples or celery, and low-fat chips and salsa.

---

5 Which Disney character is your favorite? Mickey? Daffy? Walt Disney was born on this day in 1901. Do you think *Malcolm in the Middle* star Frankie Muniz likes Disney movies? Today's his birthday, too.

---

6 Drop some hints and make a list of the ten gifts you'd most like to receive this holiday season. Then make a list of ten great gifts to give to your friends and family.

---

7 It's National Cotton Candy Day. Enjoy some of the fluffy stuff with no guilt.

---

8 Invite some friends over, grab a scroll of art paper and some paints, and create a mural. Diego Rivera, a Mexican painter known for his murals, was born on this day in 1886.

---

9 *Beauty Boost!* Have the winter beauty blues? If you're looking pale, try out some self-tanning lotion or find a blush that complements your skin tone. If your skin is dry and cracked, don't just moisturize, try out a repairing lotion.

10 Check out Amnesty International's web site at www.amnesty-usa.org and see what you can do to help in honor of Human Rights Day.

11 Build a snowman with some friends, and then come inside and drink some hot chocolate to warm your toes. Live in California? Build a sand castle and drink a cool glass of chocolate milk instead!

12 Get together with a friend to celebrate Read a New Book Month. Give her a list of your five favorite books, then ask her what her favorites are and make a point of reading them. Make sure you both suggest books the other hasn't read before!

13 *Get Involved!* Think about those less fortunate than you. Collect all of your old toys and books (or purchase new ones) and donate them to an organization that distributes them to families in need. Someone will really appreciate it!

14 *Dare Day!* Pretend for one week that you don't have a TV.

December

Party of the Month: Wrap Party

It's that time of year again—time to buy or make a ton of gifts and spend a ton of time wrapping them. So why not make a party out of it?

Invite: A small group of good friends. Have each of them bring wrapping paper and ribbon.

Dress: Casual. It's a hanging out type of night.

Decorations: Snowflakes, silver and gold streamers, snowmen, any other seasonal decorations you can think of.

Treats: Hot chocolate, holiday cookies.

Games/activities: Pop some seasonal CDs into the stereo, get all your supplies together, and wrap! Have everyone bring a grab bag gift worth ten dollars or under. Then everyone will get rewarded for her hard work.

If you're really ambitious: make your own wrapping paper out of newspaper, the funny pages, or colorful magazine pages taped together.

15 Sachets aren't just for underwear drawers anymore. Stash one in your locker, your car, or your backpack for a pleasant scent and pleasant mood all day long.

16 German composer Ludwig van Beethoven was born on this day in 1770. Did you know that he composed most of his music after losing his hearing? Pretty impressive!

It's also Chocolate-Covered Anything Day. So go for it (just stay away from insects!).

Still looking for new books to read this month? Author Jane Austen was born on this day in 1775. Pick up one of her classics, like *Sense and Sensibility* or *Pride and Prejudice*.

17 Today is National Maple Syrup Day. Have some on top of pancakes for breakfast, and be extra syrupy sweet to everyone!

18 Tons o' birthdays! Actress Katie Holmes, actor Brad Pitt, and singer Christina Aguilera were all born on this day.

Never seen *E.T.*? Even if you have, rent it in honor of one more big birthday today—the film's über-director, Steven Spielberg's.

19

Sweeten up your day by making these pretty holiday stained-glass cookies.

ingredients

one package premade cookie dough (plain)

Life Savers (or other hard fruit-flavored candy), crushed into small pieces

holiday-shaped cookie cutters

directions

1. Preheat oven to 375°F.

2. Cut dough into slices, then use a rolling pin to roll out each slice (on a counter sprinkled with flour to prevent sticking) so that it is about $\frac{1}{8}$ inch thick and flat.

3. Press cookie cutter into dough to create a shaped cookie and then transfer cookies to a cookie sheet lined with aluminum foil.

4. Using a knife, trace a smaller version of the shape in the center of the cookie. Pull out the dough from the center of the cookie, leaving only the outline of the shape. (If you'd like to use these cookies as ornaments, make a hole at the top of the shape.)

5. Fill the cut-out center of the cookie with crushed candy, until the candy is level with the dough.

6. Bake cookies for six to eight minutes or until cookies just begin to brown and candy is melted.

7. Let cookies cool on the cookie sheet. When they are completely cool, peel cookies off the foil.

8. Use cookies as tree ornaments, or eat them right away!

20 When was the last time you played a classic board game? Today—Games Day—is the day to do it. Some of our faves? Taboo, Candy Land, Mousetrap, Life, Monopoly, Pictionary.

---

21 *Dare Day!* Enter every contest you come across.

---

22 *Astrology Alert!* If you were born between today and January 20, you're a Capricorn, which means you're confident and hardworking. Your ideal love matches are Taurus, Cancer, Virgo, and Scorpio.

♑

It's the first day of winter! Why don't you try taking a break from everything to go outside and watch your breath?

---

23 *Indulge Yourself!* Spray your favorite perfume around your room.

Wanna let your angst run free? Write a poem and share it at www.teenpoetry.org.

24 *Craft Time!* Keep in touch with your friends over the winter vacation by making this stationery and writing letters. You'll need colorful stationery paper and envelopes, rubber stamps, and a stamp pad. Take a piece of the paper and decorate the top of it with the stamps. Make matching envelopes for each design. Write away!

Get Involved! Christmas Eve is your last chance to donate old toys to charity organizations sponsoring Christmas parties for less priviliged kids.

---

25 Hit the movie theaters and take advantage of all the free space today, Christmas Day. If you're celebrating the holiday, remember to help your parents clean up after everyone opens their gifts and let your siblings use your new stuff, too. After all, it's a day for giving, and not just presents!

26

"I am because we are, because we are, I am." This is the proverb most often quoted during Kwanzaa, which begins today and lasts until January 1. The holiday celebrates the past and the future, so if your family observes the occasion, study up on your heritage and tell all your relatives how much you appreciate them.

Don't forget to take a trip to the mall. It may be crazy, but the post-Christmas sales are amazing.

27

Health Tip: Drink eight glasses of water today . . . and every day! It helps keep your skin clear and glowing.

28

Rent *The Hurricane* in honor of Denzel Washington's birthday.

Dare Day! Flirt shamelessly with a boy you have a crush on.

29 Gear up for New Year's by making a list of resolutions for next year, and reflect on the past year with a list of your ten best moments.

---

30 "Nobody has a better vision of who you are than yourself." —Sheryl Crow

Indulge Yourself! Take a zillion personality quizzes today and get to know yourself even better. (Pick up the quiz book <u>What's Your Guy-Q?</u> to get yourself started!)

---

31 Tonight is New Year's Eve! Get together with friends or family and bring the new year in right!

Jada Pinkett and Will Smith had a New Year's Eve wedding in 1997. Play *Wild Wild West* after you sing "Auld Lang Syne."

Birthdays, parties, championship swim meets . . . don't forget all of your important dates! Write down any occasions you won't want to miss in your very own section for special days!

January

_____

_____

_____

_____

_____

_____

February

_____

_____

_____

_____

_____

Special Days

March

_____
_____
_____
_____
_____
_____
_____

April

_____
_____
_____
_____
_____
_____
_____

May

_____

_____

_____

_____

_____

_____

_____

June

_____

_____

_____

_____

_____

_____

_____

_____

Special Days

July

_____
_____
_____
_____
_____
_____
_____

August

_____
_____
_____
_____
_____
_____
_____

September

_____

_____

_____

_____

_____

_____

_____

October

_____

_____

_____

_____

_____

_____

_____

_____

_____

_____

Special Days

November

_____
_____
_____
_____
_____
_____
_____

December

_____
_____
_____
_____
_____
_____
_____